WHY KNOWING YOUR CALLING IS NOT THE MOST IMPORTANT THING!

BY

BISHOP OCHEI INNOCENT

Copyright reserved. No part of this book should be reproduced or copied in any way without the written permission of the author.

Contents

WHY KNOWING YOUR CALLING IS NOT THE MOST IMPORTANT THING! 1

DEDICATION 3

PREFACE 4

FIRST THINGS FIRST: WHAT IS A CALL? 6

THE HUMAN CALL: 7

THE DIVINE CALL OF GOD. 8

BY AN AUDIBLE VOICE...................9

SOME ARE CALLED WHILE IN THEIR MOTHER'S WOMB 9

SOME ARE CALLED VIA A DREAM 10

SOME ARE CALLED BY PROPHECY OR VIA A PROPHET. 12

SOME ARE CALLED VIA HUMAN AGENTS 12

SOME RECEIVE THEIR CALL BY DIVINE APPEARANCE.....................13

SOME RECEIVE THEIR CALL BY DIVINE GIFTING. 13

MANY RECEIVE THEIR CALL FROM THE GREAT COMMISSION. 15

SOME RECEIVE THEIR CALL THROUGH SERVICE 15

SOME RECEIVE THEIR CALL WITH THE ENTRANCE OF THE HOLY SPIRIT INTO THEIR LIVES. 16

SOME RECEIVE THEIR CALL BY SPECIFIC ASSIGNMENT. 18

SOME RECEIVE THEIR CALL BY MERELY FINDING THE MESSIAH JESUS CHRIST.................................18

HINDERANCES TO THE CALL..........23

SO WHERE REALLY LIES THE PROBLEM?...31

THE MOST IMPORTANT THING
ABOUT YOUR CALL.............................36

Blessings for Obedience................37

DEDICATION

This book is dedicated to the young but studious ministers of the gospel.

PREFACE

John, not real name, has received a call to start ministry for the past five to six years. He is excited about it and wearies his audience by describing in copious details how he received his call. He can spend hours talking about his call.

He is proud and excited about it but for the past years, he has done nothing about it.

Why?

He is confused: not sure he knows which area or ministry he is called into. So he sits idle as far as ministry is concerned. He even goes to the extent of daring to ask God for signs and to give God uncountable terms and conditions to further fulfill before he John can answer the call of God in his life.

Unfortunately, there are so many johns in bible schools and church pews. They sit there doing nothing while Rome, so to say, is burning.

This book examines the issue and gives life changing advice.

FIRST THINGS FIRST: WHAT IS A CALL?

Generally speaking, a call is an invitation aimed at drawing you into a duty or into discharging an assignment. It is an invitation to do something or simply to pay attention to something or just to gain your attention..

We have two major types of calls. One is the human call and the other is the divine call of God!

They are quite different from one another.

THE HUMAN CALL:
In the first case, we talk about what happens when parents and guardians give names to their child either at birth or later in life and pronounce those names when they need the attention of that child for one thing or the other. That pronouncement of the given name draws the attention of the child to the parents who now tell the child why or what they want him or her to do.

Sometimes, a human call comes in the form of a whistle or sign language. It does not really matter how the call comes. The important thing is that the person being called when that whistling sound or sign language is made, realizes that his or her attention is needed and when this attention is given, results either in a discussion or an assignment.

The call might ultimately result into an assignment or engagement.

Humans also call animals and they hear. Many give names to animals such as pets and use such names to call their attention for a specific purpose.

THE DIVINE CALL OF GOD.

This is when God is the one calling a person into his vineyard or divine assignment. This is an invitation to do the work of God. This could be in the form of an invitation to be a pioneer or helping others who have been called to pioneer new projects.

The call could be directly by God or by proxy.

There are many ways by which
God calls people to his work.
Permit me to list a few and
certainly not the only ones:

BY AN AUDIBLE VOICE.

Samuel was called via a loud
audible voice. He had it the way
we hear a preacher speaking
from the pew or the way we
hear people shout greetings at
us when passing by. This is how
the Bible puts the story of
Samuel;

SOME ARE CALLED WHILE IN THEIR MOTHER'S WOMB

Prophet Jeremiah received his
call while still in his mother's
womb. In the Bible book of the
same name [Jeremiah 1:5] we

get to hear God saying to the young and fearful Jeremiah that he has called him while he was yet in his mother's womb.

SOME ARE CALLED VIA A DREAM

God is still fulfilling His promises to date. The one below will not be an exception:

<u>Acts 2:17</u>

> *'In the last days, God says, I will pour out my Spirit on all people. Your sons and daughters will prophesy, your young men will see visions,*

your old men will

dream dreams."

<u>**Matthew 2:13**</u>

13 When they had gone, an angel of the Lord appeared to Joseph in a dream. "Get up," he said, "take the child and his mother and escape to Egypt. Stay there until I tell you, for Herod is going to search for

the child to kill

him."

SOME ARE CALLED BY PROPHECY OR VIA A PROPHET.

Elisha received his call via prophecy by Elijah. King David also received his call via prophesy which led Prophet Samuel to the house of Kish in search of a new king for Israel.

SOME ARE CALLED VIA HUMAN AGENTS

Mathew the tax collector received his call via Jesus Christ as a human. Jesus Christ was physically on earth as a human being and he invited the apostle to come and work with him. Ditto Apostle Peter. He was at sea fishing when he met Jesus Christ who extended an invitation to him to come and I will make you a fisher of men. So too several other apostles!

SOME RECEIVE THEIR CALL BY DIVINE APPEARANCE

The crucified but risen Christ appeared to Apostle Paul on the road to Damascus. The rest they say is history. From there Paul received the grace to work in the vineyard of the Lord.

SOME RECEIVE THEIR CALL BY DIVINE GIFTING.

The scripture says that God gifted Bezaliel and Oholieb for the purpose of decorating the house of God. With the gifting came the urge to use the gift and be of service to the household of God. It was after the divine visitation of the Holy Spirit to the gathered on the day of Pentecost that most of the people received the gift of boldness and the grace to speak in other languages, which equipped them to minister to persons of diverse languages. Till date, we still have testimonies of people who testify that after an encounter with the Holy Spirit they suddenly found that can minister to people of distant lands in languages they could hitherto not speak at all. This continues to happen mainly among missionaries.

**MANY RECEIVE THEIR CALL
FROM THE GREAT COMMISSION.**

Mathew 28:18-19 enjoins Christians generally to go into the nations and preach the gospel, baptizing those who accept Christ as their personal Lord and Savior.

This is sometimes referred to as a generic call to all Christians to serve. Based on this and with or without other encounters or experiences, many have answered the call of the Lord and had a great testimony.

**SOME RECEIVE THEIR CALL
THROUGH SERVICE**

Joshua was a servant to Moses. He served him faithfully and received his mantle of leadership. We also have instances where people move

with the prophets and received
the same anointing as the
prophets they serve or served
under.

SOME RECEIVE THEIR CALL WITH THE ENTRANCE OF THE HOLY SPIRIT INTO THEIR LIVES.

The Holy Spirit is like a woman. Note my words: I did not say the Holy Spirit is a woman. I am saying that he is comparable to a woman or bride.

A woman does not go to her husband empty handed. In some cultures, the bride is loaded with material gifts and attitudinal comportments as well as spiritual understandings as she heads to her new home. At worst, she comes in with her character and skin pigmentation but never empty handed.

Whenever and where ever the Holy Spirit enters into somebody, he comes laden with gifts and divine deposits.

These gifts are not given for nothing but to equip the church for service. Holy Spirit is the power that works in us for ministry and miracles: for boldness and for good success, for brokenness and holiness, etc. that enable us to serve without hesitation or reserve even in ultra hostile and provocative regions.

SOME RECEIVE THEIR CALL BY SPECIFIC ASSIGNMENT.

They are specifically called and told in clear and plain terms by God, what exactly they are to do. Jonah was told specifically to go over to Nineveh and preach repentance to them. He was left in no doubt as to what to do.

SOME RECEIVE THEIR CALL BY MERELY FINDING THE MESSIAH JESUS CHRIST.

Some of the disciples of Jesus Christ, followed Jesus Christ from the day they met him and began to do whatever he asked them to do. Mary Magdalene in the Bible followed and served Jesus Christ from the day she met Jesus Christ. There are still many like her to date.

 On earth really, there are only two sets of people:
Those who serve mammon and those who serve God! There is no middle road to stand on. Fortunately, that is as it is. God in His mercy did not leave us with multiple choices: You are either on the side of light or darkness and Jesus Christ describes Himself as the Light of the World:

"When Jesus spoke again to the people, he said, I am the Light of the world. Whoever follows me will never work in darkness but will have the light of life." John 8:12.

When you meet Christ, you migrate from darkness to light.

Jesus Christ came to this world to pay the sacred price of laying down his life for the salvation, redemption and justification of mankind and realizing that many might die without having the opportunity of hearing or know of the wonderful work Christ did on the cross of Calvary, we as followers of Christ are called into the service of witnessing this fact to the rest of mankind, teaching, baptizing and leading to Jesus Christ that they might be saved and nurtured into full understanding of the work of Jesus Christ and to mature in that understanding till they too do the same work for others.

Which is all ministry is all about!

Ephesians 4:11-16
King James Version

11 And he gave some, apostles; and some, prophets; and some, evangelists; and some, pastors and teachers;

12 For the perfecting of the saints, for the work of the ministry, for the edifying of the body of Christ:

13 Till we all come in the unity of the faith, and of the knowledge of the Son of God, unto a perfect man, unto the measure of the stature of the fullness of Christ:

On the other hand, when you have not met the saving Grace of Jesus Christ, you continue to work for the Devil or to dwell in darkness: to not only live in sin but to lure others into sin.

Most of those who serve God today do so because they met Jesus Christ. When a man or woman finds Jesus Christ, there follows a great change and liberation from serving Satan: to serving God, the Almighty.

HINDERANCES TO THE CALL

1. **IGNORANCE.** Many want to serve but they are ignorant of the call of God in their life. They have heard the emphasis and the over emphasis on the five-fold ministry as if anyone who is not sure he or she fits into any of the **"super five"**, as I choose to call them, has

no place in ministry. There are
over forty ministries in the church
of God and a person may not be
equipped or called to minister in
all.

Many ministers, even the ones
that have been years in the
ministry do not know or refuse to
accept that there are other areas
one can serve without being a
prophet, teacher, evangelist,
pastor and apostle. So when they
do not receive a call to any of these
five or do not feel a need to serve
in these areas, they begin to doubt
whether or not that have a place to
serve in the household of God.
Only ignorance can create this
avoidable situation.

2. FEAR

Many, even after they have
acknowledged the call of God in

their lives, still remain either at home or idle. One factor responsible for this is fear of the unknown and fear of failure. This in itself is a manifestation of immaturity because a mature Christian knows that it is not his work but the responsibility and Grace of God. Mature Christians know that God promised that the gate of hell shall not prevail. Mature Christians know that it is neither by power nor by might! So why should anyone be afraid.

We should be like Apostle Peter in two ways; when there was a drought and fish could not be caught all night. There appeared Jesus Christ and ordered Peter to launch out again. Despite his fears, the neophyte that he was at that point launched out in obedience

and he in-closed an abnormally
large catch! To the extent that the
net was breaking!

3. DOUBT

Doubt and fear are indeed Siamese
babies. Doubt is when we begin to
question our own ability and even
that of God. When we begin to
wonder whether God would keep
his promises. We sit there by the
table pondering and wondering
and in the end, we get nothing
done.

4. PROCRASTINATION

This is when a person who
supposed to be in ministry begins
to postpone what he or she ought
to do today to another date. We
never get to launch out because we
keep looking at the weather and
things like that.

5. THE SEARCH FOR SIGNS AND WONDERS

We are a wicked generation of wicked people who ask God for signs and wonders to prove that He is what we should know He is. We keep giving him conditions and asking for signs and in the end nothing is done while souls are out there perishing.

6. EXCUSES

This is having a good reason for not doing that which we are called to do. We have reasons that seem right in our eye but are mere tarpaulins that we try to use in covering up our disobedience. If God says "Go" and you fail to go, no matter the reason you can find or create, you are disobedient.

Unfortunately, many are not in
ministry today for no other reason
than that they are well able to
serially find excuses for not
obeying.

7. IMMATURITY

When a man or woman is
immature, he or she does not
know the time and what such time
is meant for. They may hear a call
and like the young Samuel, be
confused about who or what is
actually calling them.
That is why some who are
supposed to be ministers of the
gospel are today disc jockeys in
night clubs!

8. WRONG ASSOCIATION

It is not for nothing that we are
told in Ps 1 says: "blessed is he

that sits not in the counsel of the ungodly".
When it is time for ministry, the ungodly will certainly counsel something else.
We must all bear in mind that a married woman must not take counsel on marital fidelity from a prostitute. What association has light and darkness?

9. OLD PROPHETS

Some of us are so anxious to hold on to the little we have that those persons around us who are willing to serve are deliberately discouraged and put down. Hard as it is to swallow, I have seen such practiced in ministry. We climb and remove the ladder so that others do not climb. This happens when we consider our self interest more important than the second coming of Jesus Christ.

10.   **CHURCH POLITICS.**
We have so much time to haggle and argue that we do not have time for the things of God. The self-inflicted internal affairs of the local assembly replaces the purpose of Christian ministry and we all sit or stand akimbo watching the lost world go bye on its way to hell.

The ten points raised above do not constitute a complete list of barriers to ministry. Look around you and we see man-made and satanic road blocks springing up here and there.
The important thing is to know that these barriers are there and realize that they should not be

there at: more so where the Holy
Spirit is King.

CHAPTER THREE

SO WHERE REALLY LIES THE PROBLEM?

Many persons say that they have a call
but that the problem is that they do not

know where to start. To put it as plainly as I have heard it many times from young ministers:

They cry **"I do not know my calling."** Some say: **I know that I have a call but the problem is that I do not understand whether I am an apostle, teacher, pastor, evangelist or prophet!**

So they take this as ready excuse for doing nothing.

The situation each time I come across it reminds me of a young man in the Bible called Samuel. When he received a call from God, he could not interpret the call. So he went to an elderly priest and asked for guidance and he got the right counsel.

The young confused ministers are not helped in any way by those who insist that such person fold their hands until they get clarifications from God. Such counsel does not take Psalm 23 into counsel. Shall we take a close look at this popular psalm?

Psalm 23 (KJV)

_"The L_ORD**_ is my shepherd; I shall not want._**
2 He maketh me to lie down in green pastures: he leadeth me beside the still waters.

3 He restoreth my soul: he leadeth me in the paths of righteousness for his name's sake.

4 Yea, though I walk through the valley of the shadow of death, I will fear no evil: for thou art with me; thy rod and thy staff they comfort me.

5 Thou preparest a table before me in the presence of mine enemies:

*thou anointest my head with oil;
my cup runneth over.*

*⁶ Surely goodness and mercy shall
follow me all the days of my life:
and I will dwell in the house of
the LORD forever".*

From this psalm, we must take note of
the following we see clearly:

1. God is the one that leads. We
    should not lean on our own
    understanding.

The book of Isaiah further emphasizes
this as below:

Isaiah 30:21

*"Whether you turn to the right or
to the left, your ears will hear a
voice behind you, saying, "This is
the way; walk in it."*

2. His rod and staff are there to whip
    us into the right direction. The

shepherd's staff has a hook with which a sheep going astray is hooked and pulled back onto the right path.
This implies that even if a person goes into the wrong ministry, with time, God will use his rod and staff as our Shepherd to turn us into the right direction.

3. Therefore, we have nothing to fear. There is nothing like fear of failure or fear of mistakes. Even those who are in the right ministry also make mistakes.

CHAPTER FOUR

THE MOST IMPORTANT THING ABOUT YOUR CALL

By now, I am quite sure that it is obvious to you that the most important thing about your call is your obedience to God's call. You must make yourself available without conditions and excuses. Obedience is the foundation of Holiness and without holiness, no man can see God.

Obedience itself carries many blessings as you can see in Deuteronomy 28:1-14;-

Blessings for Obedience

28 If you fully obey the LORD your God and carefully follow all his commands I give you today, the LORD your God will set you high above all the nations on earth. 2 All these blessings will come on you and accompany you if you obey the LORD your God:

3 You will be blessed in the city and blessed in the country.

4 The fruit of your womb will be blessed, and the crops of your land and the young of your livestock—the calves of your herds and the lambs of your flocks.

5 Your basket and your kneading trough will be blessed.

6 You will be blessed when you come in and blessed when you go out.

7 The LORD will grant that the enemies who rise up against you will be defeated before you. They will come at you from one direction but flee from you in seven.

8 The LORD will send a blessing on your barns and on everything you put your hand to. The LORD your God will bless you in the land he is giving you.

9 The LORD will establish you as his holy people, as he promised you on oath, if you keep the commands of the LORD your God and walk in obedience to him. 10 Then all the peoples on earth will see that you are called by the name of the LORD, and they will fear you. 11 The LORD will grant you abundant prosperity—

in the fruit of your womb, the young of your livestock and the crops of your ground—in the land he swore to your ancestors to give you.

12 The LORD will open the heavens, the storehouse of his bounty, to send rain on your land in season and to bless all the work of your hands. You will lend to many nations but will borrow from none. 13 The LORD will make you the head, not the tail. If you pay attention to the commands of the LORD your God that I give you this day and carefully follow them, you will always be at the top, never at the bottom. 14 Do not turn aside from any of the commands I give you today, to the right or to the left, following other gods and serving them.

If you study the above scripture carefully and meditate upon it and as I will tell you from my almost three decades in ministry, all the problems, not almost all, all the problems you are fearing or procrastinating about, are small things for God to take care of. Did he not promise that He, not you, will build His church and the gates of hell will not prevail?

When God calls, we obey without delay because when we tarry, we get replaced by other willing persons that are available to God.

 We must realize that there are no shortages of messengers. God is only favoring us by giving us a great chance to serve. We must see it as a privilege and not conscription!

Even in heaven, it is implied that God gave the people the chance to accept or refuse when he asked the question:

Isaiah 6:8
"Then I heard the voice of the Lord saying, "Whom shall I send? And

who will go for us?" And I said, "Here am I. Send me!"

God did not just seize anybody. Rather, He made a call for a volunteer!

And somebody made himself available! The availability of the volunteer was sufficient for the Lord. When He calls, he equips.

He is well able to clarify your confusion and remove all fears.

Permit me at this juncture to briefly share my testimony:

My call came with a bus load of confusion because I was virtually immature. Just as I felt the hand of God upon my shoulders, I got a job offer that gave me a raise of a thousand percent! Not only that, I used to feed myself on my former pay but this new one meant that I fed three times a day at the expense of the company! In contrast, I was single and shacking in a room without conveniences but this new job came with my lone occupancy of a compound with a four bedroom flat! And so on and so forth.

In fact, the company gave me an offer I could not refuse because it was so mouth watering. I used to run around to scoop my own news. Now, the company gave me foot soldiers to run around at my beck and call.

However, it took me away, not only from my call but the church completely. I found myself in the far north of Nigeria where I was the only Christian in the set up! Each day, somebody somewhere will be playing the English version of their religious book on a centrally controlled radio and whether I wanted to or not, I was forced to listen or leave my desk.

Not only that, my chairman superiors suspecting that I might be tempted to go back to the Lagos I came from, secretly arranged for a girl from my local government area of origin to meet with me and become my sin partner. They found Samson a Delilah! I was young, naïve and without a counselor!

I almost died. I was on a business trip to Kaduna about four hundred and fifty kilometers from my base when an uprising started in Kaduna in 1992 against Christians. I escaped through the eye of a needle.

Within two weeks of that incident, I gave up the job with all the juicy pecks.

I returned to Lagos and renewed my trust in Christ. I vowed to be a better Christian. So I rededicated my life to Christ. I did not mind the fact that I was jobless.

God came to my rescue. This time instead of a secular job, I got a bigger paying job inside the church! The same editorial job that took me over a thousand, five hundred kilometers away from my home and in the midst of non-Christians but with a better pay.

Since this is not an autobiography, let me make my point. I found myself working first as a writing help to the President of a church with over a thousand branches with our headquarter church having over ten thousands in attendance on Sundays.

I believed initially that was the will of God for me.

 I went back to Bible School and over a stretch of five years, I heard God's call and just as I had informed my wife, for I married that year, that I would be resigning to take off on the assignment God had given me, the President of the ministry where I served posted me to Houston, Texas, USA! I had always wanted to go to USA and therefore, there was a great temptation.

But I believed strongly that the Lord had a different thing for me. I boldly went to the President and discussed it. It was not a disobedience. It was not a rebellion! We talked like father and son. I told him what I heard and he assured me that posting me to Houston was not "thus says the Lord" but purely an administrative decision.

He let me go. The temptation to proceed to Houston was much. The alternative was that I was stepping out to pioneer a new work from the scratch. No savings: No member. No paid work. No premises to start from.

All the same, I trusted the Lord and after prayers located a school. I walked in and talked to the proprietor. He agreed to give us a classroom for free.

We started church service on Wednesday, my wife, myself and two friends that came to pray with us. By Saturday, we started our Bible School.

To tell you the truth, I could not tell whether I was an evangelist, prophet, teacher, pastor or apostle! I just obeyed the Lord as I felt called to do. I would leave my house at nine in the morning and return sometimes as late as ten in the night. I would be in church. Sometimes I went out for evangelism.

You must know that to plant church, you have to do the work of an evangelist, prophet, pastor, teacher and even an apostle! I did them all without knowing which was my major or minor.

Within a year, we had seven small centers. I had a few wonderful testimonies of healings and prophecies coming from me. Some, I could not believe. Yet they happened.

Ministry is not about you. It is about the Owner of the work and most times, He does the miracles for His own purposes and to His Glory alone!

One day, I was in the church hall praying. With me were three adults one being a minister of the gospel. An unknown man came in. He walked up to me and greeted me. I did not know him from Adams. It was my first time of meeting him.

After the exchange of small talk, he said: "Thou man of God, thus says the Lord. Though you are doing what is necessary, it is not timely. The Lord sent me to ask you to go out into the world and strengthen pastors!"

He made some other comments and left.

I have never seen the man again even now that it is more than twenty years!

I remember that he went on to say that I would be made a bishop! Exactly ten years later, it came to pass in a mysterious way which I may not share here for now so that it will not distract from our subject.

Suffix it to state that I have seen many like me who started off without being too sure of their calling but willingly made themselves available and even in their confusion, when it seemed that they were about to go in the wrong direction our God, the Chief Shepherd would use his staff and rod, to draw them back unto the right track.

My ministry is today in several cities and countries not because I started a church but because the Lord corrected me and I went out to strengthen pastors via teaching!

When the Lord calls you, the most important thing is not dissecting the call. Rather, it is in making yourself available and where ever you are deficient, the Lord will train and equip you. Through out history, our God has never let the ship of his ministers rudderless.

Thanks and stay blessed.

THANKS ONCE MORE FOR READING THROUGH.

SHOULD YOU HAVE A NEED FOR PRAYERS, PLEASE EMAIL ME AT;
newochei@gmail.com
I ALSO ENCOURAGE YOU TO REACH ME WITH SUGGESTIONS YOU HAVE FOR THE IMPROVEMENT OF THIS BOOK IN THE NEXT EDITION.YOU CAN ALSO LEAVE AN HONEST REVIEW ON AMAZON.

ONCE MORE I THANK YOU FOR CHOOSING TO READ THIS BOOK AND I PRAY THAT ONE WORD

REMAINS IN YOU LIFE FROM THIS
LITTLE BOOK.

=BISHOP OCHEI INNOCENT.

OTHER BOOKS BY THE SAME AUTHOR

1. HOW TO DEAL RUTHLESSLY WITH THE SPIRIT OF CONSPIRACY.
2. HOW TO DEAL RUTHLESSLY WITH SIN.
3. HOW TO DEAL RUTHLESSLY WITH USE AND DUMP SPIRIT.

4. HOW TO DEAL RUTHLESSLY WITH HATRED AND RACISM.
5. SO YOU CALL YOURSELF A PASTOR?
6. SO YOU CALL YOURSELF A MANAGER?
7. SO YOU CALL YOURSELF A HUSBAND?
8. HOW TO COUNSEL A MAD MAN
9. WHY IS CHAPLAINCY NECESSARY?
10. HOW TO HANDLE REBUKE
11. HOW TO KNOW A MALCONTENT BEFORE YOU MARRY HER.
12. 2050
13. SOMETHING WORSE THAN WITCHCRAFT AND ACIDIC PRAYERS TO DESTROY IT.
14. WHY A GUEST SPEAKER MUST ASK QUESTIONS BEFORE MOUNTING THE PULPIT.

WHY MANY PROPHETS HAVE SMALL CONGREGATIONS.

ABOUT THE BOOK

In this book we will be talking about those things that render our mass and interpersonal communication on the internet woefully ineffective.

When we fail to grasp why our efforts do not produce the desired results, we keep going to the stream with a big basket.

Those who think they have an idea of what the internet is to a pastor should eat the humble pie and prepare to **learn** new ways **and unlearn** some things because there is always something new.

ABOUT THE AUTHOR

BISHOP OCHEI INNNOCENT, 64, IS THE PRESIDENT OF NEW DIMENSION SEMINARIES INTERNATIONAL.

HE IS A MEMBER OF THE INTERNATIONAL FELLOWSHIP OF THE CHRISTIAN CRISIS CENTERS, USA.

HE IS MARRIED TO LIZZY AND THEY ARE BLESSED WITH FOUR GOD FEARING CHILDREN

NOTES

NOTES

www.ingramcontent.com/pod-product-compliance
Lightning Source LLC
Chambersburg PA
CBHW051500140726
47987CB00006B/2802